# My Season of Yes!

### Breaking Your Barriers and Springing Forth Greatness Within

## Camille F. Shuler

BK Royston Publishing
P. O. Box 4321
Jeffersonville, IN 47131
502-802-5385
http://www.bkroystonpublishing.com
bkroystonpublishing@gmail.com

© Copyright – 2019

All Rights Reserved. No part of this book may be reproduced, stored in a retrieval system, or transmitted by any means without the written permission of the author.

Cover Layout: Kamaal Designs

ISBN: 9781794246850

Printed in the United States of America

# Dedication

To My Late Aunt (Dorothy Moore)
    Although you are watching from heaven, I will always remember our conversations and the fact that you saved me in my freshman year of college. It is because of your unconditional love that I am able to produce this work. I can always remember you saying, "Milly, Ca-Willy, whatever you put your mind to just keep pushing." I love you Auntie, and you will be in my heart forever!

To My Late Grandfather (Randolph Thompson)
    Hey Gramps! How are the Knicks and Yankees games watching in heaven? First, let me say that you need not to worry; Grams' is still in good hands, and we speak about you all the time. It was on Sunday afternoons; while we sat at the table for dinner, that you would encourage me and we would share our laughs. Thank you for just being you.

To My Handsome Husband (Johnny Shuler)
    Thank you for being my husband, and I am honored to be your wife. You have seen

me at my best and my worst. You have been there during my sleepless nights and my tears of joy. You are a God-sent, and I appreciate all the tough love you've shown me because you see my great potential. Thank you for pushing and praying me through every situation. I love you with all my heart.

# Acknowledgements

The words we speak should impact, inspire and encourage others. All my creativity goes to God for He only has given me the strength, bravery and ability to share this work with you. He gets all the glory and honor in everything I do.

I would like to acknowledge my parents: Bishop Lloyd Faulknor & Co-Pastor Paulette Faulknor, for always believing in me, reminding me that God + Education = Success and to always TRUST God 110%.

To my siblings: Kevin, Katerina, Cristel (RIH) and Carrece for supporting me unconditionally as well.

To my In-Loves: Rev. Charles & Earth Ferguson, Thank you for loving me unconditionally and keep all the encouragement coming.

To my spiritual parents: Overseer Jeannette Harley & Deacon Daniel Harley for pushing me in spite of my obstacles and struggles.

To my "Grams:" Mother Winnifred Thompson who continues to share with me that prayer changes anything.

To my best friend: Paula McPherson, who has always had my back no matter what!

To my publisher: Julia Royston for all your time, energy and dedication working along with me for this my 1st work.

To all my followers on social media and to everyone who feels lost, confused or ready to give up, this is for you. I love you all so much, and I crave your prayers for future projects to come.

# Table Of Contents

**Dedication** — iii

**Acknowledgements** — v

**Introduction** — ix

- Chapter 1 ~ Can I Really Do This? — 1
- Chapter 2 ~ My Adversities = My Achievements — 3
- Chapter 3 ~ Just Let Go & P.U.S.H! — 5
- Chapter 4 ~ Believe & Be Confident — 7
- Chapter 5 ~ Trusting God & The Process — 9
- Chapter 6 ~ My Thoughts & My Words Make a Difference — 11
- Chapter 7 ~ Turning My Storms into My Stepping Stones — 13
- Chapter 8 ~ I will Rise to the Top — 15
- Chapter 9 ~ Take the Leap! — 17
- Chapter 10 ~ Living in a place of Hope — 19

| | |
|---|---|
| Chapter 11 ~ Breaking My Personal Barriers | 21 |
| Chapter 12 ~ Stay Focused in the Midst of Chaos | 23 |
| Chapter 13 ~ It's Time to Celebrate | 25 |
| About the Author | 27 |

# Introduction

I wrote this book for all those individuals who has ever felt rejected and empty on the inside, but smiling on the outside. Do you remember the time when you poured your heart and soul into that one thing, and then you left it because you didn't think it or you were good enough? This book is for the individuals who need the extra motivation, zeal and drive to keep pushing. You can do this! You are stronger and wiser than you think. I pray this work breathes light and life into your situation, and that you trust God through the entire process.

This is your season to step out of your comfort zones. Will it be easy, absolutely not, but know that God is with you all of the way. Sometimes we have to go through storms in order to receive a miracle. Bishop T.D. Jakes said, "The more you are able to endure, the more you are fit for the fight." Be prepared to change your mindset and SPEAK LIFE into you! Understand that you are built for this. Never allow others to deter you from your pathway. Now, is the time to remain humble, focus on your God-given assignment, and stop giving God excuses! People are waiting to hear your story. I am praying with and for you as you embark on your journey! Pray through process of transition, the best is yet to come!

# MY SEASON OF YES!

# Chapter 1 ~ Can I Really Do This?

If you are like me, you've asked yourself several times the question, 'Can I really do this?' To be honest, even when it came to begin writing this book, I had my doubts. But as a woman of Faith, I trusted God and today I am truly excited for this accomplishment! #winning #onlyGod

Growing up we were told, "You can be anything you set your mind to." Do you remember your parent(s) or grandparents saying it? Some of us took the traditional route of going to school and getting a good job. Deep down inside you knew that you were destined for greater, but you are still making excuses. Don't worry! You are not alone, because I was there too. We need to put aside all the distractions, and do what God created us to be. The bible reminds us, "Lay aside every weight or sin which doth so easily beset us." (Hebrews 12:1) No matter if it's as simple as starting your bakery, baby-sitting business or greeting cards…you are able to be bold to push out your passion! If you are wondering can I really do this, the answer is **YES!!**

You know that you have been waiting for years to complete a specific goal or vision, and you have been procrastinating way too long. Saying Yes to your passion will motivate you to push pass all your limits and excuses! Your first step is to change your mindset. God has placed you on this earth to impact others and share your story. Now is the time to get in gear and walk the walk! I remember as a little girl, my Grams used to say, "Millie, talk is cheap, and when you put things in action is when you will get results."

Don't doubt yourself that's what the enemy wants. Take your passion and pursue it with all your heart; and I guarantee you, God will be glorified. You will be totally thrilled that someone's life will be changed by your story! The Lord is counting on you to win souls for his Kingdom. So that means, forget about what other people think about you and break down your walls. You may be afraid, nervous or even anxious; but I know that if you stay determined, you can accomplish all your heart desires. Together, we can move mountains. So, let's kick FEAR to the side and go for it! Are you ready for the adventure of your lifetime? If your answer is YES, then I encourage you to never give up and keep pushing. God and I are with you all the way!

Declaration #1: I am a WINNER and my Season of Yes is NOW!

# Chapter 2 ~ My Adversities = My Achievements

Growing up, I could remember when kids were cruel to me in my middle and high school days. They said, "You're the only black girl in our class, so you will never amount to anything." They were mean and treated me like I was a speck on the bottom of their shoes. However, I always knew in my heart that my family and God loved me. My father always told me, "If no one has a reason to give God thanks for life, it's you. No matter what anyone says, you are beautiful."

You see; as my father, he had to say those words and I just smiled. He didn't understand the hurt and pain I had to endure which began in my $7^{th}$ grade year until my senior year of high school. I was quiet and reserve, because I thought there was something wrong with me. Well, I know you may be thinking. 'You grew up where your parents were your Pastors, so why didn't you just pray about the situation?' It's a good thing you asked; however, during those times, I didn't want to share my experiences with anyone; not even my grandmother and we were very close.

The reason why I didn't go into prayer is because I didn't think God would understand back then. And if I could keep it inside and go through the motions of daily routine, then no one would become curious and ask questions. Have you ever felt that way? Can you reflect on a situation or experience where all you wanted to do is, crawl into a hole with a blanket and stay by yourself? This is a deep dark season I call my 'alone in my adversity,' because if I was alone then I can handle the difficulty on my own. To be honest; by the time I graduated from high school and was on my way to college, I had serious thoughts of suicide.

Have you ever been there at one time or another in your life? If you answered: "Yes," then let me tell you that you can rise above all your adversity and live a life of achievements and victory!! Believe it or not, you were created for so much more than just to work, pay bills and make sure your family is well. God has instilled in you purpose, destiny, vision and a plan to share with the world. Are you ready to take the leap into your untapped potential? Even if you're a little nervous like I was, don't allow your fear/nerves to override your FAITH!! God has got you covered and I have you in my prayers as well, so why are you hesitating? Let's Go!

Declaration # 2: I am an ACHIEVER, and I stand tall in my Faith!

# Chapter 3 ~ Just Let Go & P.U.S.H!

This was the hardest thing I had to do, because I had to release close family members, and friends because I had to do what God told me. Sometimes you have to isolate yourself, in order for God to speak to you clearly. Listening to God's still small voice will help you to focus on breaking your barriers. I can understand that it will hurt you to the core of your heart because I have been there, but it will be worth it in the end! Trust me! When you begin to release people out of your life that don't add value, God will begin to reveal things to you. You are more at peace in your heart and mind too. Let's take a deep breathe together. As I pray begin to remove people out of your life.

I declare and decree that you remove and delete people out of your life, so that you can tap into your God-given potential!! God is speaking expressively to your heart. And it's time to forgive yourself and go against all your struggles, so that you can change someone's life forever! Honestly, I am not saying that this will be easy, because the most difficult situations for us to endure will take a calm spirit and a strong mind.

You will have to create an atmosphere where you are in a quiet place, and God can give you specific instructions. He will connect you with the right individuals at the right time. A lot of us don't want to be free and forgive ourselves. That is a part of the process of letting go. I too didn't want to forgive myself because of my past sins, and I even fell into depression. I would smile on the outside so no one would become curious and ask questions, but I was dying and hurting emotionally on the inside.

We all may be familiar with the acronym P.U.S.H. (Pray Until Something Happens); which I believe is an excellent one, but I created Prioritize Until Success Happens. You see, please do not misunderstand what I am saying. Praying is highly important and it's the key to communication with God. Also, we need to prioritize our time and schedules to balance our lifestyle. Remember! When you completely forgive yourself, it opens a journey to your greatness within.

Declaration # 3: I Will P.U.S.H. myself into my Destiny!

# Chapter 4 ~ Believe & Be Confident

One of my favorite scriptures is, "I can do all things through Christ that strengthens me." (Philippines 4:13) When you have a vision, assignment or goal, you MUST be CONFIDENT & BELIEVE that it will come to pass. For example: Just like when you purchased your first microwave or stove, you wanted to make sure that manufacture created a product that would meet your needs. The same concept applies with our passion.

God created a gift for you to share with the world; however, you need to believe in what He has placed in your spirit to help others. Your message may not be for everyone; however, it is for someone. Barriers are blocking you to be successful. Every barrier has a core and a root. If you tackle that barrier honestly and allow God to work on your heart, your Confidence will be built up daily.

Being confident and tapping into your greatness within, changes your perspective and you have a better outcome of results. Sometimes everything may be different and that's okay; however, it will allow you to make a difference in someone's life. Confidence will take time and it will not happen overnight. I understand that it will take you outside of your comfort zone as well. Take a deep breath, because it will be a total journey. It will be worth it in the end.

The best way to make your greatness shine is to have confidence manifesting it towards others. You have to smile and believe even in your heart, if you may not be feeling 100% about the decision. I have been there and it can be a little stressful. After a day or two of thinking about the decision, you will feel more comfortable. It will be a test within your spirit, because I know it may be something that you never have done before.

This is your season to step out and take a leap of faith into the unknown. Understand that God will take you to the next level, if you just listen to his still small voice. God's voice is very clear, and he will assist on this journey called life. Continue to be who you are and know that God has your back 100%. "With confidence, you have won before you started."~ Marcus Garvey

Declaration # 4: I BELIEVE in Me!!

# Chapter 5 ~ Trusting God & The Process

If you are like me, you began the process, then life hit you and you just completely stopped. You were exhausted and didn't have the energy to continue. Did you lose motivation or thought you would never complete it? At one time or another, you were committed and excited about your passion. Then you stopped because of what other people were saying. Are you a believer that God can take you through the process smoothly?

When you are struggling to break down barriers in your life, remember God will always be with you. In the heated moment and high stress environment, I encourage you to listen to the still small voice admonishing you to go forward. I know that is easier said than done, and your saying 'Camille' you just don't understand. To be honest; I may not know the specifics of everything going on, but I do understand how it feels to throw in the towel and completely lose motivation.

When you have a vision or goal that you are passionate about, you must be willing to make the sacrifices. You may have to give up going to the game, not getting your nails done or even putting off going to your favorite movie or restaurant. Greatness is on the inside of you, and I guarantee you it will be worth it in the end.

The world is waiting on you and your gift to manifest, and for lives to be changed. STOP procrastinating and tap into your God-given assignment. Trust God throughout the entire process. Sometimes you will get down, sad or even feel like giving up, but I encourage you to trust God and leave it with Him. When negative people try to distract or deter you away from your purpose, just remind yourself that this assignment is not just for you but for everyone that will hear you! The bible says in Luke 12:48, "To much is given, much is required."

Reflection: I can remember when I decided to study law. Some people told me I wouldn't even be able to take the LSAT (the exam needed to get into law school), but I proved them wrong. If I had listened to those people I thought were my friends that said and 'claimed' they cared, I wouldn't have pushed myself to succeed. Although; I chose a different path, I am happy that my determination allowed me to push pass my limits. Are you reaching towards your highest potential?

Declaration # 5: I am TRUSTING God completely!

## Chapter 6 ~ My Thoughts & My Words Make a Difference

When was the last time you thought about your greatness within? When was the last time you broke down all your walls? Have you taken time out of your busy schedule to write down and make a strategic plan? I have realized, 'What you speak out of your mouth, that's what will come to pass.' The bible declares, "Death and life is in the power of the tongue." (Prov. 18:21)

Have you been thinking negatively or speaking negative things out of your mouth? How do you expect your passion to be produced effectively? If you are not making the necessary changes for you to be successful, you will not make a difference. Stay focused and remain humble, and everything will fall into place. My personal motto every day I say to myself is, "God has me here for a reason, so I will not be slack in doing his will." You may have even a personal motto for yourself as well. I encourage to keep saying it; and even more importantly, living it! If you need a motivation, I am here for you!

You may be in a place of being stuck or need direction, because your mind is all over the place. In a time where you may feel that way, take a step back and regroup. Believe me, you are not the only one who has been in your current situation. I can recall a time, where I was so stressed about my life that I wanted to die. Of course; I knew that was the enemy for a month straight, but I had to repeat to myself the word of God, "I shall LIVE and not DIE!! Listen! The enemy knows your weak points, and he will use anyone or anything to distract you from your assignment!

Your assignments are very critical and refuse to make excuses. Be bold, make a difference and impact the world. When you begin to see yourself becoming distracted, get back on track. The top three principles to getting back on track are as follows:
1. Clear your mind and detox daily
2. Pray that God take you through the process
3. Never give up and keep pushing.

I guarantee you. Once you do what is necessary for YOU and take full advantage of your thoughts, then everything you desire will fall into place.

Declaration # 6: I am walking in CONFIDENCE and will RENEW my mind.

# Chapter 7 ~ Turning My Storms into My Stepping Stones

Are you currently in a storm that you feel you can't get out of without drowning? I can completely relate 100%, because sometimes I was and some of you are still drowning in fear, frustration, doubt and financial struggles. Don't allow any of those storms to have you lose focus. I highly recommend that you conquer each struggle one day at a time.

The enemy is waiting for you to fail; however, God made you strong and bold enough to achieve anything! You know what? Stressing yourself out with things that you have no control over will not bring you any success. Therefore; use what you have in your hands now, and watch God open the many doors and windows of opportunity for you. Remember, that in any type of storm, God will always bring a calm. He will create an atmosphere where you break the barrier in your life and tap into the greatness within.

Are you wondering how you are going to get out of your storm? If you have answered yes to the question above, I want to share something with you. Your storm that you are going through is only temporary. It is preparing you for something better. It is only a stepping stone for your next chapter. Think about the several times your back was against the wall. You thought that you were about to lose everything including your mind, but GOD took you through the most difficult and darkest time in your life. God has not changed, and he has never failed me yet. I serve a God that is able to do abundantly above all we can ask or think.

Let me help you completely drown all your storms into the sea, shake off all your frustrations and lift your head high and move forward to pursue all your dreams. Are you ready… So, let's do it!! I will be praying with you through the process too. Remember! You may be afraid and may be alone; but that's okay, God is with you all the way. Break down every stronghold and wall that you have up right now, and show the enemy that you stepping in boldness and not allowing the storm to consume you.

Declaration # 7: My Storms don't determine my Destiny!

# Chapter 8~ I will Rise to the Top

Although things or situations in your life may be an obstacle right now, I encourage you to rise to the top! I know you may be wondering, 'Camille, how can I rise to the top?' I am so glad that you asked! First, turn your current situation over to the Lord. He is a great listener and comforter as well. Understand that what you are going through, only is a small set-back for a victorious come-back! Don't allow others to determine your destiny.

Continue to be brave and bold in your endeavors. Focus on the positive happening in your life. The bible states, "Faith without works is dead." (James 2:17) Although you may fail or get knocked down that's okay. Pick yourself up again and rise again!! Don't allow anyone or anything to distract you. You are more than a conqueror and your passion needs to be shared with others. Someone else needs to hear your story, and how God has turned your life around. You are strong and a survivor! You can be an example to other people. So, I encourage you to dry up your tears, know God and never give up. I got your back.

Giving up should not be an option for you, because you are stronger than you think. When you give up or throw in the towel, you have given the enemy the opportunity to play tricks on you and your mind. Remember! To rise to the top, you must first need to have a different mindset. Don't allow clouded thoughts to overtake your mind. Be willing to submit to God and be restored. Like me, you may be hurting from all this pain and feel like you don't want to achieve anything. If you are at this point in your life, ignore the naysayers and look to Jesus the finisher and author of your faith.

It's a process that God is taking you through. Believe me. I went though some trials and felt like no one was on my side. I felt like my spouse, friends and family just listened and tolerated me. They said they understood; but honestly, they didn't know the pain on the inside and that I cried every night just to get some peaceful rest. Rising above all your circumstances will honestly take fasting, prayer and you trusting God to take you the next level. Once you have all those above factors in place, then find an accountability partner that can push and motive you to do more. I thank God for the connections he is allowing me to make.

Declaration # 8: I will Rise to the TOP with CLASS!

# Chapter 9 ~ Take the Leap!

Leaping into your purpose or destiny can be difficult for anyone. Believe me, I have started several projects and stopped completely. Have you ever been there? Since we can relate to each other, consider taking the leap! Take the leap out of procrastination, struggles and laziness, so that you can share with the world! For years; if you are like me, you have said to yourself, "I should have… "I really want to pursue…," but never got the courage of taken the proper steps to complete the task? If your answer is yes, well I have been there too. Go ahead and forgive yourself and move forward to bigger and better things in your life!

Be able to speak positive in your life and make sure goals are aligned up with God's vision for you. Allow God to show himself strong in your life. Take the leap of confidence and faith. And I guarantee you; if you trust God completely, he will open tremendous blessings for you. Understand that it is a major risk when you take the leap, but it is worth it in the end. Is there a time when you wanted to leap, but was not brave enough? Did you ever give up way too soon? Honestly, I have and it was the most discouraging and sad feeling. I went into hiding, because I thought I couldn't handle the new adventure. I was unable to see my future as bright and didn't want to move forward.

One day I came to my Ah-Ha moment. I was sick and tired of being in this place of negativity, so

I decided to begin journaling. I am writer at heart and told God that I wanted to write the book, but never took actions steps to move forward. There were times when I felt like giving up, but this year I told God I am going to do it. I was watching a periscope on how to write a book by Carla R. Cannon, and she ignited something in me like fire!! She woke up something in my belly, and I decided to take the leap!

I am so excited that God allowed me to connect with her for this great accomplishment. When I stay focused and determined, this came to pass. I am a servant of God, and I am leaper for life! I now can encourage and motivate others to begin to leap into their purpose!! I thank God for the gift of teaching and motivating that he has placed on the inside of me. I encourage you to connect with me if you any assistance with taking the leap!!

Declaration # 9: I am ready to LEAP into my DIVINE PURPOSE!

# Chapter 10 ~ Living in a place of Hope

When was the last time you really felt hope? There has been a place where deep down inside you may have been living in H-E-L-L (double hockey sticks) as we used to say as youth. Now, your H-E-L-L may be different than mine; and that's okay, but you have you decided to get out of your comfortable surroundings. Once you heal from the major hurt and get out of your own head, you can begin the process of HOPE! Hope brings about change, victory and a new lifestyle. Are you ready to begin the journey?

Here are three things that HOPE can do for you if you are ready to commit completely.

1. Brings about change in you! You will not only be able to see the change in you, you will in others as well.
2. Claims the victory in your life. Declaring and decreeing victory in every area of your life will push you outside of your comfort zone.
3. Creates a new lifestyle. Your lifestyle and the way you carry yourself will be completely different. Your walk, talk and behavior all the way around. Even your attitude towards others will be brand new too!

I know that you may think that everything is hopeless right now, but I would like to share with you that GOD is able to change your situation. He is able to turn your life from a life of hopelessness into a life of peace and joy! Do you want to tap into the favor God has for you? Are you willing to make the sacrifices and live a happy life? If you answered yes, I encourage you to go into worship right now. Have a conversation with the heavenly father who created you and me, and let him know how you truly feel. Even though God knows how you feel, just be open and honest.

Change begins on the inside of you! You may have to delete some friends from your Facebook, Twitter, Instagram, and Snapchat in order to receive complete change. Your mindset needs to be conditioned to see the bright and excellent future that God has designed just for you. Listen, you got to turn your hopeless situation into a God-driven experience. Don't allow anyone to tell you that can't become anything, because God has given you peace, joy and mindset to change your atmosphere! I will be praying with you as begin this process.

Declaration # 10: I am CHANGING, so that God can use me!

# Chapter 11~ Breaking My Personal Barriers

I am about to be extremely transparent with you; not many individuals know about this. I have dealt with personal barriers for a long time. I didn't want to share this with anyone, because I didn't want to be judged or looked at strange. I felt broken and completely lost. I was depressed and angry that everything I wanted was not falling into place. Yes, I knew how it pray, but I didn't want to because I thought God was not listening.

I was out there all alone, until I decided to pick up the phone and call my Auntie Moore; may God rest her soul. She always encouraged me, and I can remember her saying, "Milly-Cawilly, just take your time. God will not fail you." I shared with her that I had major thoughts of suicide, because nothing was falling into place. I was not confident at all. In my mindset, I was nothing and not good enough. After much encouragement and love from my family and friends, I chose to LIVE!! I told myself that God has a greater assignment for me to do!

You too may have personal barriers that need to be broken. If so, I want to encourage you to seek God; the creator, and he will help you through this tough process. God will never leave you nor forsake you, because that's what his word says. As you break down the barriers, you will feel so FREE!! All the anger, stress and frustration will be removed. The pain is real and tiresome. The pain will hurt you to the core, and may even put you in isolation for few days. I'm just being honest. This process is horrible, but it will make you STRONGER! You will have VICTORY AND TRIUMPH after this!! You will be able to share your story with others, who are in the same dysfunctional state right now. Just keep calm and remember God is able to take you through anything.

Declaration #11: My FOCUS will lead to my Future!

# Chapter 12 ~ Stay Focused in the Midst of Chaos

It was in the midst of all the chaos all around me, where I had to shake myself loose of everything. I had to dry up all my tears, and tell God I am ready to be used. You may be in a place just like I was, and you feel like no one loves or understands you. You feel like ending your life and just having PEACE in your mind, heart and spirit. Listen, I have been there, and I was ready to throw in the towel. I wanted to let you know that in the midst of your chaos, you need to remain focused.

You may want to know, 'How do I stay focused with everything crashing down all around me?' Great question! Here are 5 Ways you can stay focused:

- ❖ Take a deep breath, God has your back!
- ❖ Trust God 110% throughout the process!
- ❖ Learn that your failures are just a set up for your favor!
- ❖ Speak LIFE into your situations!
- ❖ Never Give Up. God has greater in store for you!
- ❖ Bonus: Speak daily affirmations to yourself and watch God work out miracles for you!

Once you have completed the above successfully, you will able to change your mindset, live a life of abundance and become more happier in your spirit! Sometimes we become overwhelmed with life, and that's okay. But if we keep our minds, focus on our goals and never allow anyone or anything to deter us from our dreams, we will make it!

Now, write down your top 5 steps that you will take towards staying focused.

1._____

2._____

3._____

4._____

5._____

Declaration #12: My FOCUS will lead to my Future!

## Chapter 13~ It's Time to Celebrate!!

Yes, yes, yes!! It's time to celebrate YOU!! You have made it through some struggles, disappointments, sleepless nights and even some failures; however, God brought you through them ALL!! Thank you Jesus and (insert praise shout/dance) NOW!! You have a reason to give God all the glory and honor because I know you are thinking, 'How did I make it out that situation too?'

The amazing and exciting news is that you don't need to ask for anyone's permission to have JOY, PEACE and HAPPINESS all over! I am rejoicing with you as you read! I am so glad that you took time out to assess who you are, and NOW it's time to have a party!! It may be a party in your home, heart or even the back yard, but it's time to have a BLAST!!

Take time out, step back and think about where God has brought you from. You could have been dead, in a mental hospital or etc, but LOOK @ GOD!! He turned it! (in my Tye Tribbett's voice!!). Never give up on you, and never forget that you can make it through any storm, test or situation that the enemy places in your way.

Keep your head up high and smile although you may be hurting, and I guarantee you that you will have VICTORY, PEACE, TRIUMPH and SUCCESS on the other side!! I love you so much, and you know where to reach me when you need me!!!

Write down your top 3 BEST moments to remember them! #YesGod #Conqueror

1. _____
   _____

2. _____
   _____

3. _____
   _____

>   Declaration # 13: I will CELEBRATE ME EVERYDAY!!!

## About the Author

Camille F. Shuler, The Mindset Motivator, she motivates, educates, and coaches everyday individuals on how to live a life of pure freedom through strategic coaching and dynamic speaking.

Camille always had a passion to write from a young age, and as she got older, she understood that it was her passion. Writing allowed her to relieve some stress as well.

Camille is the CEO & Founder of Camille Shuler Ministries since 2015, and she has impacted people's lives every day since. She is determined to do what God has called her to do and will not stop until He instructs her on how to do it too.

To find out more about Camille, visit www.CamilleShuler.com

Made in the USA
Middletown, DE
22 January 2019